The QUEST for
BASKETBALL'S PERFECT SHOT

SWISH

MARK STEWART AND MIKE KENNEDY

MILLBROOK PRESS · MINNEAPOLIS

The following images were provided by the Authors: Naismith Memorial Basketball Hall of Fame, pp. 6, 11; YWCA USA, p. 8 (bottom); Murad Tobacco, p. 10; Capital Cards, p. 12; Spalding Sporting Goods, p. 13; Sheboygan County Historical Research Center, pp. 18, 19 (bottom); Bowman Gum Co., p. 19 (top); Editions Recontre S.A., p. 21 (top); Topps, Inc., pp. 21 (bottom), 29 (bottom), 33 (bottom); Collegiate Collection, pp. 23 (top), ; Courtside Collection, pp. 23 (bottom), 25 (bottom); From the Authors' Collection, pp. 25 (top), 31 (bottom); Duke University, p. 26; Classic Games, Inc., p. 27 (both); Fleer Corp., pp. 29 (top), 50; WNBA Enterprises, LLC, p. 31 (top); General Mills, Inc., p. 33 (top); The Nera Collection, p. 40.

The following images are used with the permission of: © iStockphoto.com/Joachim Angeltun, pp. 1, all backgrounds; © Ronald Martinez/Getty Images, p. 4; © Hulton Archive/Getty Images, p. 8 (top); © Nathaniel S. Butler/NBAE/Getty Images, pp. 9, 41 (bottom), 49 (bottom); © Wen Roberts/NBAE/Getty Images, pp. 14, 59 (top); © NBA PHOTOS/NBAE/Getty Images, pp. 15, 48, 53; © Focus on Sport/Getty Images, pp. 16, 34, 42, 58, 60 (top); © Rich Clarkson/Time Life Pictures/Getty Images, p. 20; © Rich Clarkson/Getty Images, p. 22; © Getty Images, p. 24; © Andrew D. Bernstein/NBAE/Getty Images, pp. 28, 39, 44, 52, 54; © Jim Gund/Getty Images, p. 30; © Scott Cunningham/NBAE/Getty Images, p. 32; © Walter Iooss Jr./NBAE/Getty Images, pp. 35, 45; © Noah Graham/NBAE/Getty Images, p. 36; © George Gojkovich/Getty Images, p. 37; © Rocky Widner/NBAE/Getty Images, pp. 38 (top), 62; © Bill Baptist/NBAE/Getty Images, p. 38 (bottom); © Layne Murdoch/NBAE/Getty Images, p. 41 (top); © Ron Hoskins/NBAE/Getty Images, p. 43 (top); © Wen Roberts/AFP/Getty Images, p. 43 (bottom); © Fernando Medina/NBAE/Getty Images, p. 46; © Robert Lewis/NBAE/Getty Images, p. 49 (top); © Ernest Sisto/New York Times Co./Getty Images, p. 55; © Rick Stewart/Getty Images, p. 56; © Jen Pottheiser/WNBAE/Getty Images, p. 57; © Kent Horner/NBAE/Getty Images, p. 59 (bottom); © Barry Gossage/NBAE/Getty Images, p. 60 (bottom).

Front Cover: © Glenn James/NBAE/Getty Images (top); © iStockphoto.com/Joachim Angeltun (bottom); © Andrew D. Bernstein/NBAE/Getty Images (cover flap, left); © Rick Stewart/Getty Images (cover flap, right).

Special thanks to Nera White and Brenda Hiett

Unless otherwise indicated, the memorabilia photographed in this book is from the collection of the authors. The logos and registered trademarks pictured are the property of the teams, leagues, and companies listed above. The authors are not affiliated with any of these organizations.

Millbrook Press
A division of Lerner Publishing Group, Inc.
241 First Avenue North
Minneapolis, MN 55401 U.S.A.

Website address: www.lernerbooks.com

Library of Congress Cataloging-in-Publication Data

Stewart, Mark, 1960–
    Swish : the quest for basketball's perfect shot / by Mark Stewart and Mike Kennedy.
        p.   cm.
    Includes index.
    ISBN: 978–0–8225–8752–1 (lib. bdg. : alk. paper)
    1. Basketball—United States—History—Juvenile literature. 2. Basketball players—United States—Juvenile literature. I. Kennedy, Mike (Mike William), 1965– II. Title.
GV885.1.S74 2009
796.3230973—dc22   2008024958

Manufactured in the United States of America
1 2 3 4 5 6 – DP – 14 13 12 11 10 09

Contents

Introduction

One of the sweetest sounds in the world is the SWISH a ball makes as it brushes against the thick cords of a basketball net. This sound can mean only one thing: a player has made a shot, and a team has added to its score.

A basket might be the reward for a total team effort. It might be the result of one player's talent. It might just be a lucky shot. Indeed, no two baskets are exactly alike. A ball can travel many different paths from a shooter's hand into the net. Making a basket is limited only by a player's skill and imagination.

Basketball began in the United States more than one hundred years ago. Since then, the sport has spread all over the world. New players and new ideas come to basketball every day. This book looks at the art of shooting and how it has shaped the game. Most of all, it celebrates the special thrill you get from launching a shot and watching the ball—and listening to it—as it swishes through the basket.

Manu Ginobili floats a soft shot over the outstretched arms of two defenders in the 2005 NBA Finals. A player has many ways to put the ball in the basket.

1 *Aiming for the Stars*

THE HISTORY OF SHOOTING

You don't have to be a sports fan to know that basketball is very different from other games. It looks different, sounds different, and requires different skills than other sports. Basketball is different in another important way. No one is exactly sure when or how those other sports began—or even who invented them. We do know these things about basketball.

In the autumn of 1891, students at the YMCA Training School in Springfield, Massachusetts, were facing another dreary winter of indoor exercise. In the fall and spring, they played fun outdoor sports such as baseball, football, soccer, and lacrosse. However, when the weather turned cold, they were stuck inside in the gymnasium. They marched, did calisthenics, and twirled wooden clubs shaped like bowling pins. Boring!

The school wanted to create a new team sport that would keep students active and entertained indoors. An instructor named Dr. James Naismith came up with

A group of men play a game they called basket-ball outdoors in 1892.

Dr. James Naismith

a game he called basket-ball. He posted a set of thirteen rules for his new sport before class on the morning of December 21. His students decided to give basket-ball a try. They loved it.

One day, teachers from a nearby women's school saw the young men playing basket-ball. Their students started playing too. Before long others learned about this challenging new game. Soon basketball spread all over the country.

Naismith later admitted that basketball could have ended up being called crate-ball or box-ball. He had asked the school's janitor, Pop Stebbins, for two square crates to nail up at either end of the gym. Pop did not have any. Instead, he offered Naismith two round peach baskets. A round ball and a round basket? It made sense to Naismith, and the rest is history.

Players and fans didn't hear any SWISH-ing in the early years of basketball. Not until 1893 were wooden baskets replaced by iron rims and nets. Another twenty years passed before the modern net was invented and the first true SWISH was heard. Still, the thrill of making a perfect shot—and the excitement of inventing a new one—helped fuel enthusiasm for the United States' newest game.

By the early 1900s, men and women were playing basketball in almost every U.S. town. The game was perfect for gyms, dance halls, theaters, armories, and field houses. These buildings had large floors and

As this YWCA poster shows, basketball was a popular game for women at the turn of the century.

Girl Power

Women have been playing basketball, unlike other sports, for as long as men. Women compete at every level, from grade school to professional leagues. The "mother" of women's basketball was Senda Berenson. She was a teacher at Smith College in Massachusetts. In the 1890s, most people believed that playing sports was bad for the health of young women. Berenson disagreed. She thought basketball was an excellent game for her students.

In 1899 the Spalding sporting goods company asked Berenson to write the official rules of women's basketball. They were different from the men's rules. Players were not allowed to run up and down the entire court. They had to stay in certain zones. Also, there was a limit to the number of times a player could dribble. Berenson's rules made passing and shooting very important parts of the women's game. Not surprisingly, some of the finest shooters in the country during that time were women.

For the next sixty years or so, women continued to play basketball according to these rules. Six players took the court for each team. Three played offense only, and three played defense only. They did not cross half-court (the area where a line separates the court in two equal halves). This restriction kept the best players from showing all their "modern" skills. By the early 1970s, the women's game finally began to change. Women played five-on-five just like the men. Free to display all their talent, the top stars proved just how good they could be.

At the same time, the women's game was growing in popularity in Europe and Asia. Several countries started professional leagues. During the 1980s and 1990s, many U.S. college stars played overseas after graduating.

The first successful U.S. pro league started after the 1996 Olympics. The U.S. team (*above*) had won the gold medal, and fans everywhere were very excited about women's basketball. The Women's National Basketball Association (WNBA) began play in 1997. Over the years, the world's best players joined the league. They helped focus even greater attention on the teamwork, energy, and skill that characterize the women's game.

high ceilings, which provided plenty of room for players and fans. In big cities, meanwhile, playgrounds were hard to find. Churches and settlement houses responded by converting their big basements into basketball courts.

Back then basketball was a rough game that caused a lot of bumps and bruises. Referees called fouls only when players were hit very hard or knocked off their feet. Players wore thick pants and pads on their knees and elbows to protect themselves.

Basketball grew quickly in popularity after 1891. The first trading cards appeared in 1911.

Nets or wire cages surrounded many courts, which prevented players from spilling into the audience as they chased after a loose ball.

Basketball was also a very fast game. Players darted back and forth and passed the ball all over the court. Dribbling the ball was not yet important. The ball at the time was large and heavy. It also had laces, like a football, so it did not always bounce straight.

Making a basket was not easy. Many players were still learning the basics of the game. They took almost all shots with two hands. Some players launched the ball from behind their heads, much the way soccer players toss balls from the sidelines. The most popular style of shooting was a two-handed shot from the waist or chest. Very few shots actually went into the basket. Most points were made on free throws, which were awarded to a player who had been fouled.

Slowly but surely, players found different ways of putting the ball in the basket. In U.S. high schools and colleges, coaching became more important. Coaches started sketching out plays for their teams. They taught their players how to get shots at the basket without defenders blocking their vision. As more and more people across the country began to understand and appreciate basketball, the game grew in popularity.

Many young immigrants—and the children of immigrants—began playing basketball as well. The United States was a melting pot of many ethnic groups during the early 1900s. Basketball offered them an opportunity to meet other young people from the same homeland who spoke the same language and had the same customs. In that way, the sport helped immigrants realize they were not alone in their new country.

At the same time, basketball also made immigrants feel more American. The sport had been invented in their new home, and they took pride in being part of something that the United States could claim as its own. The groups that excelled in basketball

Players take the court for South Dakota's state high school tournament in 1923.

included German Americans and Irish Americans. The sport was also popular among Jewish people who had come to the United States from Russia and eastern Europe.

Most children of immigrants were too poor to go to college. Fortunately, the best players found ways to continue playing basketball as they got older. Many joined teams that were part of professional leagues. Basketball became their job. A good player could make anywhere from five to fifty dollars a game, which was a good salary in those days. Players also made money coaching school teams. High school and college students soon caught on to the "tricks" of the pros.

Throughout the 1920s, sports of all kinds grew in popularity in the United States. The top basketball players started to become famous. The best-known team was the Original Celtics. New York was their home, but they traveled all over the northeast. The Celtics started as an all-Irish team but soon welcomed players from many different ethnic groups. The best players in the country wanted to play for the Celtics. Over the years, many of them did.

The leader of the Rens, William "Pop" Gates, was one of the best athletes in the country. Gates was also a professional baseball player.

The top college players of the 1920s did not play professional basketball after they graduated. Most found jobs in one business or another. When they played basketball, it was strictly for fun. A few of those players decided to become coaches. They taught younger players what they knew and spent countless hours dreaming up new ways to put the ball in the basket.

During the 1930s, the United States went through the Great Depression (1929–42). Many people lost their jobs. They could not afford to buy tickets to support a professional basketball team. Most pro leagues went out of business. Still, fans loved basketball and wanted to enjoy the sport. College basketball became extremely popular during this time.

Players who continued to play professionally joined teams that traveled from town to town. The Celtics were one such team. So were the Harlem Renaissance, or "Rens." The Rens were an all-African American team. Wherever the Celtics or Rens played, everyone who watched them tried to copy their moves.

At the same time, several large companies formed their own teams. They played one or two games a week against other companies. Fans loved to watch these games. Workers were happy when their company could say it was the best in basketball. Putting a strong team on the court was also a smart way for a company to advertise its products and services. Some of the best U.S. teams belonged to department stores, grocery stores, factories, and car dealers.

In the 1940s, company teams continued to play and helped form a number of professional basketball leagues. The Detroit Pistons, for example, started as a team for a factory that made pistons (parts that help make engines work). Other pro teams from this time were called the Jeeps, Jets, and Gears.

Basketball went through many changes during this growing period. In the sport's rough-and-tumble early days, players chose to keep both feet on the floor at all times. That was

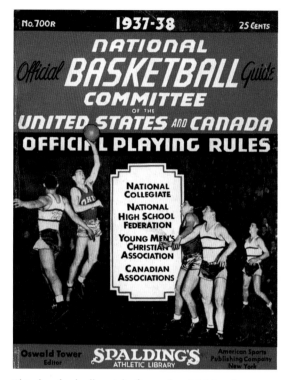

This basketball guide from the 1930s shows a player releasing the ball while in the air. This was a new shooting style at the time.

because a player jumping in the air could easily be shoved off the court without a foul being called. In the 1930s and 1940s, the game "took off." Players shot while in the air and on the run. The fast break became a popular weapon. And the role of the center became very important, because a tall player could grab rebounds and make quick passes over the heads of opponents to help teammates get open shots.

Modern basketball was finally taking shape. Players continued to experiment with shooting techniques and other new strategies. In the years after World

Going Pro

Since the early 1900s, men's professional basketball has gone through many changes. From the 1920s to the 1940s, the two top leagues were the American Basketball League (ABL) and National Basketball League (NBL). Many teams in these leagues also played games against

other teams to make extra money. In 1946 the Basketball Association of America (BAA) formed. Three years later, the BAA merged with the NBL to become the National Basketball Association (NBA). For nearly two decades, the NBA was the only professional league for men.

In 1967 the American Basketball Association (ABA) began and tried to compete with the NBA. The ABA was known for its entertaining and imaginative players. In 1976 the ABA went out of business, but four of its teams joined the NBA, which grew to twenty-two teams. The NBA welcomed a host of new stars, including Julius Erving, David Thompson, and Connie Hawkins (*left*). Since then the NBA has added eight more teams to bring the total to thirty.

For women, professional basketball got its first big break in 1978, when the Women's Pro Basketball League (WPBL) formed. For the first time, women had a coast-to-coast league. The WPBL lasted only three short seasons.

Much more important to the women's game was a new law (Title IX) passed in 1972. It forced colleges to create women's teams in nearly every sport that had a men's team. Women's basketball flourished in the 1980s and 1990s. The best players joined pro leagues in Asia and Europe, because no league existed in the United States. Soon there was enough talent in women's basketball to start three professional leagues, the American Basketball League (ABL), National Women's Basketball League (NWBL), and the WNBA. The ABL and the WNBA were rivals for several years, while the NWBL was considered more of a minor league. Although there were plenty of good women players, there were not enough fans to support three leagues. In 1999 the ABL went out of business, and its best players joined the WNBA. In 2007 the NWBL also went out of business. The WNBA grew to fourteen teams. It is the most successful women's major league in the history of pro sports.

MEN'S PRO LEAGUES	
ABL	1925–26 to 1930–31
NBL	1937–38 to 1948–49
BAA	1946–47 to 1948–49
NBA	1949–50 to Present
ABA	1967–68 to 1975–76

WOMEN'S PRO LEAGUES	
WPBL	1978 to 1980
ABL	1996 to 1999
NWBL	1997 to 2007
WNBA	1997 to Present

War II—which was fought from 1939 to 1945—there were enough good players and enough fans for new professional leagues to start. At the same time, college basketball was becoming more popular than ever.

In 1949 two leagues joined forces to form the National Basketball Association (NBA). Initially, the NBA struggled to attract fans. The players were big, strong, and tough. They worked hard for every shot—and just as hard to stop every shot. A team could control the ball for an unlimited amount of time. Often one team would "stall" and wait for an easy shot. The result was low-scoring games. Basketball fans grew bored with the NBA. By the early 1950s, many had given up on the league.

In 1954 the NBA made a key rule change. Each team was given just 24 seconds to shoot the ball. After 24 seconds without putting up a shot, a team lost possession of the ball. A "shot clock" was placed near the court so players knew how much time they had to shoot. The extra passing and dribbling that slowed the game down suddenly disappeared—teams simply didn't have enough time to play the old way.

Bob Pettit rises for a layup. He was one of the stars who helped make the NBA more exciting in the late 1950s.

A new kind of player soon took over. He did not have to use a trick play or get a perfect pass in order to find an open shot. Instead, he "created" his own shot by driving to the basket or jumping in the air. He would release the ball before a defender could block his shot. The age of the superscorer had begun. Basketball games became faster and more exciting. Scores went up every year as

Thanks to players like Julius "Dr. J" Erving, the dunk is now basketball's most popular shot.

players discovered new ways to put the ball in the basket.

By the 1960s, pro and college basketball looked very much like the game you see currently. Before long, the sport ranked as one of the United States' favorites. Soon, basketball spread all over the world. As bigger, stronger, and faster athletes picked up the game, basketball soared. Players used their talent and imagination to build on the success of those who came before them.

In the twenty-first century, players standing seven feet tall have become midair acrobats. Players under six feet tall win dunking contests. Women have become a vital part of basketball too. They have taken the fundamentals of the game to a higher level than the men!

Players have found more ways to swish a basketball than anyone could have imagined just a generation ago. It makes you wonder what Dr. James Naismith would think of his creation—and what today's players would think of him. What would they do if he showed up at a playground with a funky, laced ball in one hand and a peach basket in the other?

Do you think they would call him Doctor J?

2 Buzzer Beaters

AMAZING GAME-WINNING SHOTS

The clock is ticking down. Your team is losing by a point. The fans are on their feet and cheering as loud as they can. Who's going to take the last shot?

Some players love the pressure of basketball's most intense moment. When their team needs a basket with only seconds remaining, they want the ball in their hands. Others end up heroes by accident. The ball finds them with time running out. They simply do what comes naturally—focus on the rim and shoot for the victory.

Basketball history has countless stories of dramatic "buzzer beaters"— game-winning shots taken just before the final horn sounds. The ball floats through the air for only a second or two. But to the players and fans, it can seem like a lifetime. When the shot swishes through the hoop, the memory lasts forever.

What are basketball's greatest buzzer beaters ever? The following pages look at some of the best. Read on and join the debate.

Sheboygan Shocks the Pistons

MARCH 29, 1943 • FORT WAYNE, INDIANA

In the spring of 1943, some basketball players were overseas fighting for the United States in World War II. Others stayed behind to work in factories making things important to the war effort, including guns, tanks, jeeps, boats, and ammunition. Many of those players joined the National Basketball League, which was the top U.S. professional league at the time. They worked during the day and played games at night and on weekends.

The 1942–43 NBL Finals matched the Fort Wayne Zollner Pistons (who later became the Detroit Pistons) and the Sheboygan Redskins. The first team to win two games would take the James Naismith Memorial Trophy.

The teams split the first two games. The final game took place in Fort Wayne's small, noisy arena. The Pistons led most of the way, but the Redskins stayed close. Sheboygan trailed 28–27 with time running out.

Eddie Dancker (22) stands tall in this team photo of the Sheboygan Redskins from the 1940s.

Redskins guard Buddy Jeannette brought the ball upcourt and passed to center Eddie Dancker. Dancker was 25 feet from the basket. He surprised everyone by launching a long hook shot. The ball banked off the backboard and swished through the hoop!

The Redskins were NBL champions. Dancker's shot gave fans something to talk about for years to come. It was the first—and only—time that a pro championship was decided on the final basket.

Collector's Corner

BUDDY JEANNETTE

Jeannette joined the Redskins in the middle of the 1942–43 NBL season and gave the team a trusted leader. He was one of the first player-coaches to win a pro basketball championship. Jeannette was elected to the Basketball Hall of Fame in 1994.

1948 Bowman Buddy Jeannette card

SHEBOYGAN REDSKINS

The Redskins played for the NBL championship five times in six seasons during the 1940s. The team name honored the Native Americans of the team's home state, Wisconsin.

1940s Redskins uniform patch

19

The Soviets Grab Gold

SEPTEMBER 10, 1972 • MUNICH, GERMANY

From the mid-1940s to the early 1990s, the United States and the Soviet Union were enemies. Although the two countries never fought each other directly in a war, they often battled in the Olympics. In 1972 the Americans and Soviets met on the basketball court. The winner would receive a gold medal. The loser would settle for silver.

The U.S. players are in shock as Aleksander Belov raises his arms in triumph after his last-second basket.

The Soviet team held a 49–48 lead late in the game. They fouled U.S. star Doug Collins with only three seconds left. Collins made two free throws to give the United States a 50–49 lead. The Soviets quickly passed the ball inbounds for a desperate shot. At the same time, coach Vladimir Kondrashin signaled for a timeout, and the referee stopped the action.

Kondrashin called his players to the bench and gave them a play. The Americans were ready for it and stopped the Soviets. The Americans believed they had won. But Kondrashin argued that the clock had not been reset

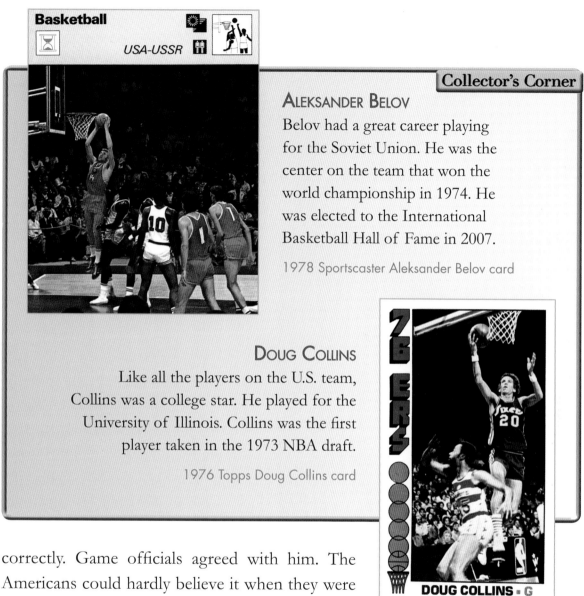

Collector's Corner

ALEKSANDER BELOV

Belov had a great career playing for the Soviet Union. He was the center on the team that won the world championship in 1974. He was elected to the International Basketball Hall of Fame in 2007.

1978 Sportscaster Aleksander Belov card

DOUG COLLINS

Like all the players on the U.S. team, Collins was a college star. He played for the University of Illinois. Collins was the first player taken in the 1973 NBA draft.

1976 Topps Doug Collins card

DOUG COLLINS · G

correctly. Game officials agreed with him. The Americans could hardly believe it when they were ordered back onto the court.

This time, the Soviets made the winning basket. Aleksander Belov caught a long pass and hit a layup to win the game. The U.S. players were so angry that they refused to accept their silver medals. In 1991 the Soviet Union broke up into many smaller countries. The United States developed good relations with these countries. Fans, however, still argue about this game all these years later.

Jordan Hammers the Hoyas

MARCH 30, 1982 • NEW ORLEANS, LOUISIANA

When one basket means the difference between winning and losing a championship, a coach has a hard choice to make. Who takes the big shot? Dean Smith had many options at the end of the 1982 National Collegiate Athletic Association (NCAA) Championship game. The University of North Carolina Tar Heels had Sam Perkins, James Worthy, and Jimmy Black on the court. All were talented and experienced players.

The Georgetown University Hoyas were ahead 62–61 with 32 seconds left. They had a strong and confident defense led by Patrick Ewing. As the Tar Heels passed the ball around looking for an open shot, the Hoyas guarded Worthy and Perkins closely. They left a nineteen-year-old freshman open on the left side, nearly 20 feet from the basket.

No one knew it then, but that skinny teenager was the last player

Michael Jordan watches the ball after releasing his game-winning shot.

the Hoyas should have left unguarded. His name was Michael Jordan. He took a pass from Black, rose off the floor, flicked his wrist, and sent the ball on its way. It swished through the basket to give North Carolina a 63–62 lead.

Moments later, Georgetown's players were still in shock from Jordan's unexpected basket. The Hoyas threw the ball away, and the Tar Heels won the championship.

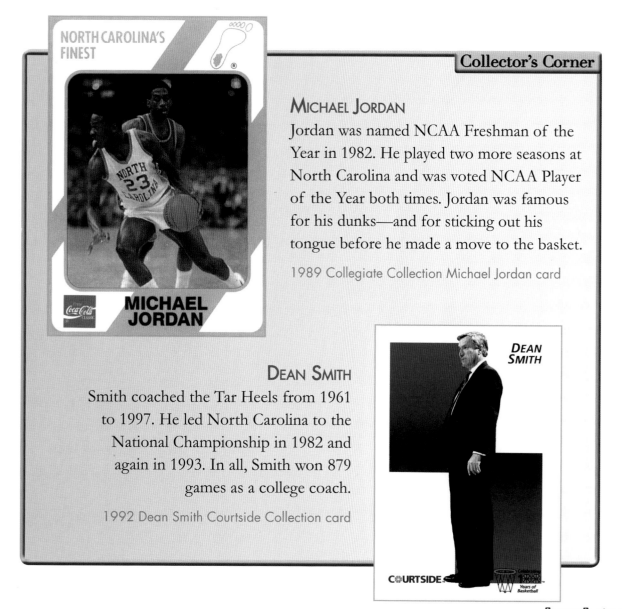

NORTH CAROLINA'S FINEST

MICHAEL JORDAN

Collector's Corner

MICHAEL JORDAN
Jordan was named NCAA Freshman of the Year in 1982. He played two more seasons at North Carolina and was voted NCAA Player of the Year both times. Jordan was famous for his dunks—and for sticking out his tongue before he made a move to the basket.

1989 Collegiate Collection Michael Jordan card

DEAN SMITH
Smith coached the Tar Heels from 1961 to 1997. He led North Carolina to the National Championship in 1982 and again in 1993. In all, Smith won 879 games as a college coach.

1992 Dean Smith Courtside Collection card

DEAN SMITH

COURTSIDE

Lorenzo's Slam Sinks Houston

APRIL 4, 1983 • ALBUQUERQUE, NEW MEXICO

During the 1980s, the slam dunk became basketball's most popular play. No college team was better at it than the University of Houston. The Cougars were led by superstars Clyde Drexler and Hakeem Olajuwon and coached by Guy Lewis. Before Houston met the North Carolina State University Wolfpack for the 1983 NCAA Championship, Lewis joked that the team with the most dunks would win.

How right he was! Jim Valvano, the coach of the Wolfpack, told his players to keep the Cougars away from the basket—and from dunking. Late in the second half, the score was tied 52–52. Neither team had made a dunk.

With time running out, the Wolfpack passed the ball around waiting for the final shot. Houston nearly stole a pass to

Coach Jim Valvano shows the world who's number one after the Wolfpack's amazing victory.

Dereck Whittenburg, who panicked and tossed up a jump shot from 30 feet away. His teammate, Lorenzo Charles, saw the ball falling short and grabbed it out of the air. Without coming down, he turned and stuffed the ball in the basket. The Wolfpack won the championship, 54–52, on the first dunk of the game.

LORENZO CHARLES

Before the championship game, Jim Valvano told Charles that he was not playing up to his potential. After making the winning dunk, Charles became a star for the Wolfpack. He averaged 18 points a game in his last two college seasons.

Lorenzo Charles signed floorboard

JIM VALVANO

Valvano was one of college basketball's smartest and funniest coaches. He once asked a referee if it was against the rules for thinking something bad about him. The referee said, "No." Valvano smiled and said, "Well, I think you stink." They both had a good laugh . . . and then the referee called a technical foul!

1992 Courtside Collection Jim Valvano card

Christian Laettner
Shoots Down Kentucky

MARCH 28, 1992 • PHILADELPHIA, PENNSYLVANIA

Duke University and the University of Kentucky have played many memorable games. Fans will never forget when the Blue Devils and Wildcats squared off in the 1992 NCAA tournament. The winner would move on to the Final Four. The loser would go home.

The game was very close. The score was tied 93–93 at the end of 40 minutes. Near the end of the 5-minute overtime period, Sean Woods made a basket for Kentucky. The Wildcats led 103–102 with 2.6 seconds left. Duke coach Mike Krzyzewski called timeout and sketched out a play for the Blue Devils.

Grant Hill (33) rushes to congratulate Christian Laettner on his remarkable shot.

Grant Hill threw a long pass from near his own basket. Christian Laettner caught the ball near the Kentucky foul line. Wildcats were on both sides of him. He spun to his right and then quickly spun back to his left. Just as Laettner hoped, the Kentucky defenders backed away. He rose into the air and swished a 15-foot shot to win the game.

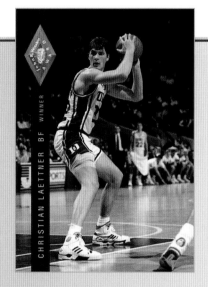

Collector's Corner

CHRISTIAN LAETTNER

Laettner led the Blue Devils to the NCAA championship in 1991 and 1992. He was at his best at tournament time. Laettner was named College Player of the Year in 1992. He went on to play thirteen seasons in the NBA.

Classic Games Christian Laettner card

GRANT HILL

Hill is a talented all-around player. In 1991 he made an amazing dunk against the University of Kansas. It was one of the greatest shots ever in an NCAA Championship game. In his first NBA season, Hill received more votes for the All-Star Game than any other player.

Classic Games Grant Hill card

Paxson Puts the Suns on Ice

JUNE 20, 1993 • PHOENIX, ARIZONA

Basketball is a team sport—even if a teammate is one of the greatest players ever. The Chicago Bulls proved this in Game 6 of the 1993 NBA Finals. The Phoenix Suns led 98–96. They were 14 seconds away from tying the series.

The Bulls passed the ball to Michael Jordan. Everyone thought he would take the last shot. They were wrong. When two Phoenix defenders met Jordan, he passed the ball to Scottie Pippen. The Suns quickly blocked his path to the basket. Pippen passed the ball to Horace Grant, who was just a few feet from the basket.

Grant was a good shooter, but John Paxson was better. While the Suns were chasing the Bulls, Paxson had quietly moved to his favorite spot behind the three-point line.

John Paxson's Chicago teammates have already started celebrating as he launches his game-winning shot.

Grant turned and whipped a pass to Paxson. He rose and released a smooth jump shot that found the bottom of the net. A few seconds later, the Bulls were celebrating their 99–98 victory. They were world champions for the third time in a row.

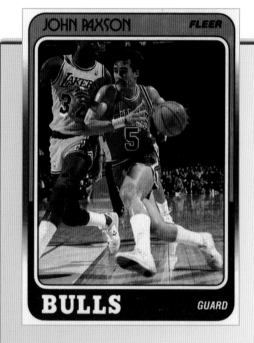

Collector's Corner

JOHN PAXSON

Paxson was a true sharpshooter. He made 15 of 24 three-point shots during the 1993 playoffs. Paxson became the general manager of the Bulls in 2003. Paxson's father and brother (Jim Sr. and Jim Jr.) also played in the NBA.

1991 Fleer John Paxson card

HORACE GRANT

Grant was one of the NBA's best defensive players. He was also a good rebounder and scorer. Grant has a twin brother Harvey who also played in the NBA.

1992 Topps Archives Horace Grant card

Tech Gets Caught in Charlotte's Web

APRIL 3, 1994 • RICHMOND, VIRGINIA

When less than one second remains in a game, a player must catch the ball and shoot it in one lightning-fast motion. Sylvia Hatchell, coach of the University of North Carolina Tar Heels, made sure her players knew this. They trailed Louisiana Tech University 59–57 in the 1994 NCAA Championship game. The clock read 0.7 seconds—time for one last desperate shot.

Hatchell wanted her 6' 5" center, Sylvia Crawley, to take the shot. But Louisiana Tech guarded her closely. Instead, Charlotte Smith got the ball. Smith was standing more than 20 feet from the basket when she caught the inbounds pass from Stephanie Lawrence.

Charlotte Smith launches her buzzer beater an instant after receiving a teammate's pass.

The ball barely touched Smith's fingers before she launched a long three-pointer. The ball swished through the hoop to give North Carolina the championship.

INDIANA FEVER
CHARLOTTE SMITH

CHARLOTTE SMITH

Like her uncle David Thompson—who was an NBA superstar in the 1970s and 1980s—Smith was a great scorer and leaper. She had 23 rebounds against LSU in the 1994 championship game. A year later, she dunked during a game.

2007 WNBA Enterprises Charlotte Smith card

SYLVIA HATCHELL

Hatchell became coach of the Tar Heels in 1986. She was elected to the Women's Basketball Hall of Fame in 2004. Hatchell won her 500th game with UNC during the 2007–08 season.

Sylvia Hatchell signed floorboard

Jordan Hits a High Note

JUNE 14, 1998 • SALT LAKE CITY, UTAH

Michael Jordan had already won five NBA championships when the Bulls took the court against the Utah Jazz in Game 6 of the 1998 NBA Finals. The Jazz wanted to win badly. They had played well in the series but trailed three games to two. Even so, Utah was confident it could win Game 6 and take the championship in Game 7.

With less than a minute left, the Jazz had the ball and the lead, 86–85. A victory was within their grasp. John Stockton passed to Karl Malone, but Jordan got his hand on the ball. He made the steal and dribbled toward the Utah basket. Bryon Russell was waiting for him near the three-point line.

Bryon Russell turns to watch as Michael Jordan releases his game-winning shot.

Russell was a good defender. When Jordan faked to the basket, Russell stayed with him, but Russell's foot slipped just a bit. That was enough for Jordan to fire a twenty-foot jumper. He swished it to give Chicago an 87–86 victory. With his final shot as a Bull, Jordan won his sixth championship.

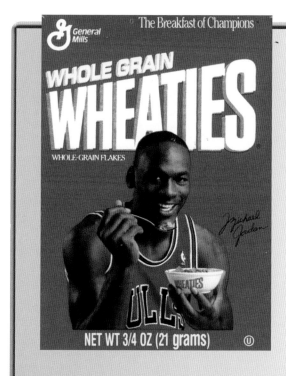

MICHAEL JORDAN

Jordan was voted the Most Valuable Player (MVP) of the NBA Finals after each Chicago championship. In 179 playoff games, he averaged 33.4 points a game.

Michael Jordan snack-sized Wheaties box

BRYON RUSSELL

Russell was very good at guarding players far from the basket. Few players besides Jordan would have even tried to beat Russell with a jump shot. Many Utah fans believe that Jordan pushed Russell, but Russell says there was no foul.

2001 Topps Bryon Russell card

3 *Sensational Scorers*

THE ART OF SHOOTING

A player has many ways to score a basket. Some players like to shoot from far away, while others prefer layups and slam dunks. Great scorers are good at several shots, but almost every player has a favorite. This chapter explores the most popular shots in basketball and the players who made them their own.

SET SHOT

The set shot is basketball's oldest shot. The shooter sets both feet on the floor and then launches the ball toward the basket. In the early days, players took set shots with both hands and released the ball from chest height.

One of the best set shooters ever was Bobby McDermott. He often made baskets from 30 feet or more—far beyond the current three-point line. In 1950 McDermott was voted the greatest player in history.

Of basketball's modern players, Larry Bird was a great set shooter. Bird played in the 1980s and 1990s. He shot with his right

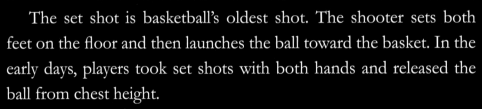

Larry Bird aims his set shot. He used the same shooting style at the free throw line.

hand and used his left hand to steady the ball as he brought it back over his head. Bird was a master of almost every shot, so defenses never knew what to expect from him.

The set shot is still a very important part of women's basketball. One of the best at it is Katie Smith, a veteran star in the WNBA. She sets her feet quickly and launches the ball next to her right ear. Smith is hard to stop because she can repeat each shot with the same easy motion.

ONE-HANDER

By the early 1930s, many players had begun experimenting with one-handed shots. To make up for the power they lost by using just one hand, they jumped toward the basket. A college player named Hank Luisetti became very good at making one-handers while running. He would dribble past his man, leap off the floor, and then shoot before the defense had a chance to block the shot. Luisetti's style would lead to the jump shot, which almost every current player uses.

Oscar Robertson rises above the defense to shoot his famous one-hander.

Even as the jump shot became popular, a number of players continued to shoot one-handed. The best was Oscar Robertson, who often jumped away from his defender instead of toward the basket. His shot was beautiful to watch and impossible to block. Robertson was also an excellent passer and rebounder. During the 1960s, many fans believed he was the NBA's best all-around player.

George McGinnis followed Robertson a decade later. He was a big, powerful forward who shot one-handed while attacking the basket. McGinnis was a scoring champion and MVP in the ABA during the 1970s.

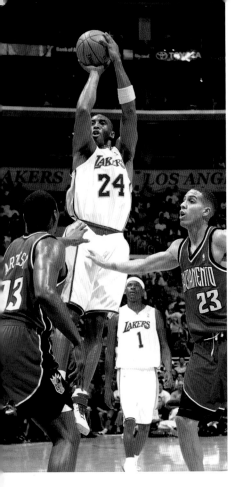

Kobe Bryant shoots a jumper. He uses his right arm to aim his shot.

Another famous one-handed shooter was Magic Johnson, the leader of the Los Angeles Lakers in the 1980s. Johnson was known for his dribbling, driving, and passing. But when a defense left him open, he could pop in one-handers from 25 feet.

JUMP SHOT

Basketball changed forever when players began using the jump shot as a major weapon. A good jump shooter can make baskets at any time, from any place on the court. Most of the game's great scorers have had good jump shots.

Not everyone shoots a jumper the same way, but the basics are the same. A player jumps in the air, uncoiling the body and arms to transfer the energy of the leap into the wrists and fingertips. At the top of the jump, the player releases the ball—making sure to line up the eyes and shooting arm with the target.

One of the first great jump shooters was Paul Arizin. He learned to shoot in the 1940s in a gym with low ceilings, so his jump shot had very little arc. Another early jump shot artist was Whitey Skoog. He tucked his legs underneath him when he shot.

Jerry West had one of the prettiest jump shots of the 1960s and 1970s. He was at his best when dribbling to the basket and then suddenly springing in the air to take his shot.

During the 1980s, two of the best jump shooters in the NBA were Kiki Vandeweghe and Chris Mullin. Both believed that practice makes perfect. Vandeweghe and Mullin took hundreds of jumpers a day, so every shot felt natural during a game. In recent years, Glen Rice's form on the jump shot was as close to perfect as any in history.

Ray Allen and Gilbert Arenas could "stop-and-pop" from anywhere on the court. Kobe Bryant is another amazing jump shooter. His jumper is one of the most accurate ever. It helps make him one of the greatest players the NBA has ever seen.

MID-RANGE JUMP SHOT

The mid-range jump shot may look easy during warm-ups, but it is difficult during games. A player takes the shot from about 15 feet away from the basket. Defenders often converge on this area, so the shooter has little room and little time to rise off the floor. The key is to release the ball quickly, because one or two opponents may be close enough to block the shot. A mid-range jump shooter must also have a feathery-soft touch or the ball will rattle out of the basket.

A player's size is not important for making a mid-range jump shot. In the 1960s and 1970s, guards such as Hal Greer, Dave Bing, and John Havlicek were good at this shot. So were forwards during this period, including Tom Heinsohn, Billy Cunningham, Adrian Dantley, and Alex English.

The mid-range jump shot can also be a weapon for undersized centers. Willis Reed used it against the great defensive centers of his era, including Bill Russell, Wilt Chamberlain, Nate

The great Kareem Abdul-Jabbar is helpless against Bob McAdoo's mid-range jump shot.

Thurmond, and Wes Unseld. Bob McAdoo's mid-range shot was very unusual. He brought the ball far behind his head before letting it fly. He led the NBA scoring and was the 1975 league MVP.

In recent years, as NBA players have become taller and faster, fewer have made the mid-range jump shot a part of their game. One star who continues to favor it is Richard Hamilton. He swishes mid-range jumpers just like the old-timers did.

Allen Iverson angles toward the basket as he drives past a defensive player.

THE DRIVE

Every player has a different way of driving to the hoop for a layup or dunk. Smaller players often start from far out and dart past two or three defenders. Bigger players often start closer to the hoop and use power moves to get to their target.

One of the best "little men" was Nate "Tiny" Archibald. He was a lightning-quick ball handler who could dribble right past his defender. Archibald led the NBA in scoring and assists in 1972–73.

Like Archibald, Allen Iverson also loves to score against bigger, stronger players. He has a brilliant crossover dribble that completely confuses defenders. Iverson was the NBA scoring leader four times and was named the league MVP for the 2000–01 season. Chris Paul has followed in Iverson's footsteps. He is so fast going to the hoop that opponents have to focus all of their attention on him.

Pete Maravich was bigger than Archibald, Iverson, and Paul, but he had more moves than anyone when it came to driving to the hoop. He looked as if he was making up shots as he was taking them. And sometimes he was!

Big men with a talent for driving included George Mikan, Walt Bellamy, David Robinson, and Shaquille O'Neal. Mikan—the NBA's best player in the 1950s—was a rough center who used his hips and elbows to back his man toward the basket. Bellamy was a star in the 1960s. He liked to wait for a defensive player to make his move

Cynthia Cooper rises toward the rim.

and then dribble, spin, or jump past him to the rim. Robinson was a gymnast as a boy. Although he grew to seven feet tall, he was graceful and quick enough to glide past most defenders during his prime in the 1990s. O'Neal uses his great power and size to get to the hoop. The NBA's most rugged defenders often look helpless when they try to guard Shaq.

Driving to the basket is also a key part of the women's game. One of the best ever at this skill was Cynthia Cooper. She exploded toward the basket for layups or passes to open teammates, but she always played under control. Cooper led her college team to the NCAA Championship in 1983 and 1984 and helped Team USA win a gold medal in the 1988 Olympics. She joined the WNBA at the age of thirty-four and was named MVP in the league's first two seasons. Cooper's drives helped the Houston Comets win the league championship four years in a row.

SLAM DUNK

Of all the shots in basketball, the slam dunk is the closest to a sure thing. A player jumps high in the air and then throws the ball down into the basket with one or two hands. Players began dunking the ball in

LeBron James soars to the rim on his way to a thunderous dunk.

the 1930s but rarely during games. It was considered bad sportsmanship. For many years in college basketball, dunking actually was against the rules. By contrast, the NBA found that dunking was a great way to attract fans.

In the 1960s and 1970s, stars such as Elgin Baylor, Connie Hawkins, Julius Erving, and David Thompson played basketball "above the rim." Baylor was never the tallest man on the court, but he could usually jump the highest. When he had a clear

Air Nera

Nera White (*left*) was the first true superstar in women's basketball. In 1958 White led a team of U.S. women to the World Basketball Championship. She won ten amateur championships as well.

White stood 6' 1" and thrilled fans with her soaring rebounds and drives to the basket. She was a great scorer who had a deadly hook shot and an accurate 25-foot jump shot. Another of her specialties was sinking baskets from half-court. White also had amazing leaping ability. Every so often, she would rise to the rim and dunk the ball, bringing the crowd to its feet.

path to the basket, all opponents could do was watch him fly past them. Hawkins had enormous hands. He could control the ball in one hand as he soared through the air. In his first year in the ABA, Hawkins led the league in scoring and his team won the championship. Erving also starred in the ABA. He was nicknamed Dr. J because of the way he "operated" on the court. Erving could score from anywhere, but his acrobatic dunks were the most exciting part of his game. Thompson stood only 6' 4", but he could touch the top of the backboard. No wonder he was called Skywalker.

These players paved the way for the dunking specialists of the 1980s and 1990s, including Dominique Wilkins, Clyde Drexler, and Larry Nance. Wilkins slammed the ball down with tremendous force. He was a quick and powerful player who loved to finish the fast break. Drexler was a silky-smooth scorer who made the game look easy. His nickname was Clyde the Glide. Nance was long and lean. He could bend and twist his body in the air and use his long arms to dunk from many different angles.

Tim Duncan is one of the "kings" of the bank shot.

Almost every player currently in the NBA can dunk. One of the best is LeBron James. When he sees an open lane to the basket, he explodes toward the rim and jams the ball into the basket.

BANK SHOT

Bank shots have been around as long as there have been backboards. Rather than trying to shoot the ball directly into the basket, a player aims for a spot on the backboard, so that the ball bounces off it and into the hoop. To understand the angles of different bank shots, a shooter must practice from almost every part of the court.

When basketballs had laces, bank shots were very popular. When balls without laces were introduced, shooting directly into the basket became much easier. However, a few players continued to use the backboard on their shots.

Sam Jones and Rudy Tomjanovich were bank shot artists. Jones was one of the top scorers on the Boston teams that won nine NBA championships in the 1960s. Tomjanovich was a forward who played for the Houston Rockets during the 1970s. More recently, center Tim Duncan has proven that he knows all the angles too. His shooting helped the San Antonio Spurs win three championships in five years.

FADEAWAY

When a player jumps away from the rim, the chances of making a basket usually go down. Some players, however, are actually better shooters when they "fade away" from the basket.

Karl Malone "fades away" against long-armed Scottie Pippen.

The best at the fadeaway shot—including Elvin Hayes, Michael Jordan, and Karl Malone—were great shooters to begin with. Hayes was one of the NBA's top scorers and leaders in the 1970s. Jordan and Malone followed him a decade later. The ability to drift backward when shooting made these players even harder to stop. All three were known for their desire to attack the basket. That meant that defenders usually were ready to back up when guarding them. By fading away, Hayes, Jordan, and Malone guaranteed they would have a clear look at the rim.

TURNAROUND JUMP SHOT

Many shooters use a turnaround jump shot to confuse a defender. The shot is taken just as its name suggests. The shooter backs toward the defender and then spins left or right to release the ball toward the hoop. If opponents can only see the shooter's back, they can never be sure when a shot will be launched—or which way a shooter will turn.

Making a turnaround jumper takes strength, balance, and agility. A player spinning in midair must be able to locate the basket, estimate its distance, and then take the shot in less than a second.

The first great turnaround jump shooter was Joe Fulks. In the 1940s, while some players were experimenting with jump shots, Fulks could spin left or right, spring into the air, and launch the ball toward the basket. During the 1950s, George Yardley was the master of the turnaround jumper. He became the first NBA player to score 2,000 points in a season.

Another NBA star with a great turnaround jump shot was Bernard King, the league's scoring leader in 1984–85. When King had the ball with his back to the basket, his defender tried to guess which way he would turn. If his opponent guessed wrong, King

Bernard King spins and shoots before three defenders can react.

WNBA fans watch Lisa Leslie fire a turnaround jumper.

dribbled to the basket for a layup or dunk. If he guessed right, King's turnaround jumper was still good enough to go in.

The turnaround jump shot is also a good weapon for big men who play close to the basket. Kevin McHale and Patrick Ewing used their long arms and great body control to make the turnaround jumper an unstoppable weapon.

The turnaround is a very effective shot in women's basketball too. Many centers use the shot after they receive a pass with their back to the basket. In the WNBA, Lauren Jackson and Lisa Leslie have scored many of their baskets this way.

FINGER ROLL

One of the most graceful shots in basketball is the finger roll, which a player takes very close to the basket. Players with long fingers and great jumping ability are especially good at this shot. The shooter stretches out toward the rim and flips the ball up and into the basket with the fingers.

Two masters of the finger roll were Wilt Chamberlain and George Gervin. During the 1960s, Chamberlain used the finger roll instead of the dunk when a defensive player was in his way. He simply jumped toward the rim, reached out over his opponent's head, and dropped the ball through the hoop. In the 1970s and 1980s, Gervin used the finger roll on his drives to the rim. He would hold the

Wilt Chamberlain towers above defenders as he rolls the ball into the basket.

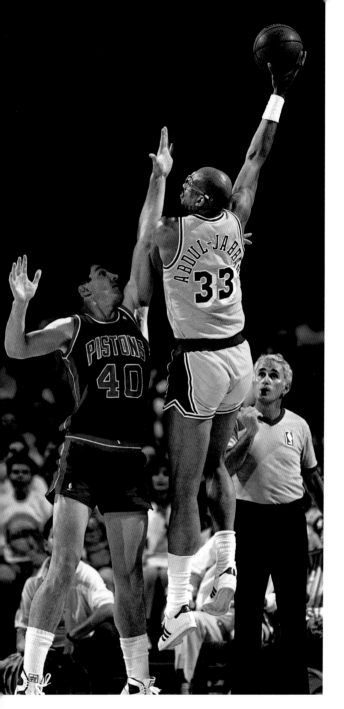

Bill Laimbeer has no way of blocking Kareem Abdul-Jabbar's "sky hook."

ball out and wait until a defender tried to swat it out of his hand. At the last moment, he would flick the ball over his opponent's hand and into the basket.

HOOK SHOT

What is the best way for a shooter to keep an opponent from blocking a shot? By using the body to shield the ball from the defender. That simple idea led to the hook shot. A player flips a soft shot with an arching movement over the defender's outstretched hands—and into the basket.

One of the first great hook shooters was center Neil Johnston. He used the hook to lead the NBA in scoring in 1954–55. A smaller player known for his hook shot was Cliff Hagan. He played in the same era as Johnston. With his running hook, he could score against opponents who were much taller. During the 1970s, Bob Lanier used his big body to move close to the hoop. He then dropped short hooks right into the basket.

No one had a more famous hook shot than Kareem Abdul-Jabbar. He stood over seven feet tall and had long arms. Abdul-Jabbar released his shot so high that he could shoot down at the rim. He retired in 1990 as the NBA's all-time leading scorer.

The free throw (or foul shot) is "free" because no one is allowed to defend against it. That does not mean it is an easy shot. When standing at the free throw line after being fouled, a player's heart is pounding, and the body is aching. Making a free throw takes great composure and focus—especially when a game is on the line.

Two of the best free throw shooters were Bill Sharman and Dolph Schayes. Both were all-stars in the 1950s. Sharman was a perfectionist. He practiced this shot hundreds of times a day. Schayes could shoot from anywhere on the court, but he had a lot of practice from the "charity stripe" because he was fouled so often.

Rick Barry, the NBA's Rookie of the Year in 1966, shot his free throws underhanded. While young fans thought this looked weird, older fans remembered that almost everyone shot underhanded until the 1940s! One of the best free throw shooters was Calvin Murphy, a star in the 1970s who was also one of the smallest players in history. That was an advantage at the foul line, because his shorter limbs made it easier to have a consistent shooting motion.

Many of the NBA's tallest players, in fact, have been poor free throw shooters because of their long arms and legs. But

Rick Barry prepares to shoot a free throw underhanded.

that's not the case for Yao Ming and Dirk Nowitzki—two of the tallest players in the NBA today. When Yao was a teenager in China, he practiced free throws every day. Nowitzki, who grew up in Germany, learned his smooth shooting style when he was a young guard. By the time he unexpectedly grew to seven feet, he had already perfected his free throw shooting motion.

A three-pointer is on its way, courtesy of Reggie Miller. When Miller retired in 2005, he held the NBA record with 2,560 three-point shots made.

In recent years, Steve Nash has been one of the NBA's best free throw shooters. He was named the league's Most Valuable Player twice. When the game comes down to free throws, Nash is the player teammates want on the line.

THREE-POINTER

The three-point shot has been a part of pro basketball since the 1960s and in college ball since the 1980s. The distance on a three-point shot is different in the NBA (just under twenty-four feet) and men's college basketball (just under twenty feet). The same is true in the WNBA (just under twenty-one feet) and women's college basketball (just under twenty feet).

Since the ball travels farther on a three-pointer, a shooter's motion must be perfect and the body must be lined up exactly right. Three-point specialists over the years have included Louie Dampier, Mark Price, Byron Scott, Dale Ellis, Jeff Hornacek, Reggie Miller, Peja Stojakovic, Michael Redd, and Ben Gordon. All were excellent all-around players too. Opponents often backed off them because they could also drive to the hoop. When that happened, it was usually bombs away!

4 Longest, Shortest, Weirdest, Wildest

BASKETBALL'S MOST REMARKABLE SHOTS

How many ways are there to make a basket? Just when fans think they have seen it all, a player does something that no one has ever done before. One of basketball's most famous shots took place way back in 1908. The University of Chicago and the University of Wisconsin were tied 16–16. Pat Page had the ball for Chicago with time running out. A much larger defender trapped him. Page hooked the ball over his head, hoping to pass to another Chicago player. Instead, the ball swished into the basket to win the game.

Chicago fans were still talking about that shot when the University of Pennsylvania came to town a short time later. During a scramble for a loose ball, Page grasped it with two hands but could not straighten up because of the Pennsylvania players surrounding him. He looked between his legs and saw an open teammate. Page "hiked" the ball like a football player. His desperate pass sailed over his teammate . . . and went right into the basket. Chicago won the game 21–18.

In the century since Page's famous shots, a lot of strange things have happened on the basketball court. Sometimes, good luck plays a part. In a preseason NBA game in 1969, Donnie May of the New York Knicks did not see a pass coming from a teammate. The ball bounced off his head and landed right in the basket. Sometimes, bad luck leads to 2 points—for the other team. In a 2007 NBA game, Luke Walton of the Los Angeles Lakers lost his grip on the ball after grabbing a rebound. The ball popped in the air and went into his own basket.

Luck wasn't involved in the weird shots Rod Hundley made. He spent as much time practicing trick shots as he did regular ones. In the 1950s, when his college team was way ahead, Hundley liked to put on a show for the fans. Sometimes he shot free throws with his back to the basket, and sometimes he shot from his knees. In the NBA, Hundley also made free throws with a hook shot. When Hundley was on the floor, fans stayed in their seats hoping to see what Hot Rod would do next.

Sometimes, a seat for a basketball game should come with safety goggles. In the days when backboards were made of glass, slam dunks could get messy. Big, strong players slamming the ball into the basket would occasionally shatter the backboard. What a mess! Pieces of glass would shower the court—and anyone sitting nearby. The first NBA player to destroy a backboard was Chuck Connors of the Boston Celtics. He did it during warm-ups before the team's first game in 1946.

"Hot Rod" Hundley shows one of his unusual shooting techniques.

NBA star Gus Johnson shattered three backboards during his career. During the 1960s, Johnson made the windmill dunk famous. He would cradle the ball as he drove to the basket and then whip his arm in a circular motion over his head before dunking. Charlie "Helicopter" Hentz also liked to swing his arms when he dunked. He destroyed two backboards in one game in 1970.

Darryl Dawkins takes it easy on this dunk.

Spencer Haywood, another star of that era, smashed a backboard in his first college game. The arena had no replacement, so Haywood's team was declared the winner. Darryl Dawkins shattered two backboards in 1979. He was very pleased with himself, but the NBA was not happy. After Dawkins broke the second backboard, the league installed new collapsible rims and threatened to fine players who tried to repeat Dawkins's feat.

One of the strongest players—and dunkers—in history was Charles Barkley. Though he stood only 6' 5", Barkley was a great leaper with a powerful body. Sometimes when Barkley wanted to dunk, he jumped too high. In one game, he had three dunks waved off by the referees. Each time the ball bounced off his head—which was right under the hoop—before it went through the net and then popped back out of the basket. The rules say that a basket does not count until the ball goes through the bottom of the net.

Michael Jordan usually had no trouble dunking the ball, though he did get help on his most famous slam. At the end of the movie *Space Jam*, Jordan tries a game-winning dunk from half-court. When evil aliens stopped him, computer animators stretched his arm the rest of the distance so he could make the shot.

Although fans love to watch players dunk, the most exciting shots are desperate, last-second tries from far away. One of the most famous long shots came during

Charles Barkley completes a powerful dunk.

the 1957 NBA All-Star Game. Bill Sharman of the Celtics heaved the ball from 70 feet and swished it at the buzzer. His teammate, Bob Cousy, had made a 79-foot shot in a game three years earlier. That was the NBA record for many years. Norm Van Lier of the Chicago Bulls broke it with an 84-foot shot. Later, Baron Davis of the Charlotte Hornets made an 89-foot shot.

Of all the long shots in history, the most remarkable may be a 60-footer by Jerry West of the Los Angeles Lakers. It came during the 1969–70 NBA Finals and sent a hard-fought game into overtime.

The NBA did not have a three-point rule back then, but the ABA did. During the ABA's first season, Jerry Harkness of the Indiana Pacers heaved a 92-foot shot at the buzzer with his team behind 118–116. The ball banked into the basket for three points and an amazing victory. Despite his heroic effort, Harkness was later cut from the team. The reason? He did not have a good outside shot!

Long Shots

The player best known for his long shots was Meadowlark Lemon (*below*), the star of the Harlem Globetrotters in the 1960s and 1970s. The Globetrotters are not part of any professional league. They travel around the world playing exhibition games. The Globetrotters thrill fans with their comedy and tricks, but there was nothing tricky about Lemon's shooting. During each game, he would try a hook shot from half-court. Over the years, Lemon made far more than he missed.

The best half-court shot in recent memory came during a game between the Los Angeles Clippers and Cleveland Cavaliers. While the players were taking a break at halftime, a member of the Clippers Spirit dance team swished a shot from 45 feet with her back to the basket. The crowd cheered longer and louder for her than any player that night, including superstar LeBron James.

5 *Fabulous Feats*

AN INSIDE LOOK AT SCORING

Believe it or not, a basketball rim actually has enough space inside to fit two balls. That does not mean that scoring a basket is easy. It takes years of practice, plus great skill and imagination. And when another player is trying his hardest to keep the ball out of the basket, making a shot can seem like the most difficult thing in the world to do.

During his long career, Michael Jordan made fewer than half the shots he tried. Yet no one in history scored more remarkable baskets. Fans first saw his amazing talent during his freshman year in college when he helped the University of North Carolina win the 1982 NCAA Championship. That was just the first chapter in the legend of Michael Jordan.

A few years later, Jordan was doing amazing things in the NBA. He was the league scoring champion ten times. Many of those points came on baskets that people are still talking about. During the 1985 NBA playoffs, Jordan and the Chicago Bulls faced the Boston Celtics. In the second game of the series, Jordan took control.

He made long three-pointers and spectacular dunks—and every other kind of shot. When the final buzzer sounded, he had scored 63 points!

In 1991 Jordan and the Bulls won their first championship. During the NBA Finals, he made a shot that stunned the players and fans. Jordan drove to the basket for a right-handed dunk. Sam Perkins of the Los Angeles Lakers rose to block his shot. Just as Perkins tried to swat the ball, Jordan calmly switched the ball from his right hand to his left hand as he hung in the air. Then he banked in a layup for two points.

Michael Jordan and his Chicago teammates celebrate one of their six NBA championships.

A year later, Jordan was at it again. This time the Bulls were playing the Portland Trailblazers for the NBA championship. In the first game, Jordan let the Blazers know who was in charge. He scored 35 points in the first half, including six three-point shots. After making his sixth long bomb, he turned to the crowd, shrugged his shoulders, and smiled. Even Jordan was amazed by his own shooting.

Jordan was not the first player to make an unforgettable shot while playing for a championship. During the 1980 NBA Finals, Julius Erving of the Philadelphia 76ers made a basket that still has the Lakers shaking their heads. Erving drove down the right baseline and lifted off for one of his famous dunks. He had just one problem: Kareem Abdul-Jabbar moved in front of the basket to block his shot.

Erving simply glided past the 7' 2" center—and then past the rim—before reaching around the opposite side and spinning a shot off the backboard and into the basket. Magic Johnson of the Lakers remembers thinking, "Should we [keep playing,] or should we ask him to do it again?"

The Lakers had their fair share of great scorers. When they played in Minneapolis, their star was George Mikan. He stood 6' 10" at a time when most players were barely over six feet. Teams were always looking for ways to stop Big George. Even the NBA tried. The free throw lane used to measure just six feet across. The current lane is twice as wide. The NBA made the change to keep Mikan from standing too close to the basket. In 1948 the Lakers played the New York Rens in the finals of the World Professional Basketball Tournament. The Rens had a great defense, but Mikan scored 40 points in an exciting 75–71 victory.

Ten years later, Bob Pettit had a memorable game when his St. Louis Hawks played the Celtics in the NBA Finals. In the final game, Pettit attacked

During the 1950s, George Mikan was an unstoppable scorer in the NBA.

the basket again and again. He scored 50 points, including the winning basket with 15 seconds left. No one has ever scored more points in a championship game.

Isiah Thomas drives to the basket against the Lakers.

Scoring in the playoffs is a lot harder than scoring in the regular season. Teams play extra-tight defense, and the pressure is incredible. One of the best playoff scorers was Jerry West of the Lakers. His nickname was Mr. Clutch because he loved to take (and make) his team's most important shots. In the 1965 playoffs, West averaged 46 points a game against the Baltimore Bullets. In the 1969 NBA Finals, he shot so well against the Celtics that he was named the Most Valuable Player—even though his team lost!

Another player known for his scoring in the playoffs was Isiah Thomas. He was often the smallest man on the court, but when he got hot, no one could stop him. During the 1988 NBA Finals, Thomas scored 25 points in one quarter against the Lakers. In 1984 against the New York Knicks, Thomas exploded for 16 points in 93 seconds.

The Knicks also had their hands full with Reggie Miller of the Indiana Pacers. He was a great scorer who saved his best for the fans in New York. During the 1994 playoffs, Miller scored 25 points in a quarter against the Knicks. One year later, he scored 8 points in the final 9 seconds to produce a win over New York.

Bill Walton dominated Memphis State University in a similar way during the 1973 NCAA Championship game. Walton played center for the University of California

Wilt Chamberlain leaps high above the Knicks for a loose ball. They could not stop him the night he scored 100 points.

at Los Angeles (UCLA). He was a great passer and shot blocker. Against Memphis State, he was also a scoring machine. Walton took 22 shots and made 21 of them, plus two free throws. He finished with 44 points, and his Bruins were the kings of college basketball.

A great scorer does not have to take all of his team's shots. Two of the best shooters in history were great passers too. Rick Barry was the top scorer in college basketball, then in the NBA, and finally in the ABA. He always thought of himself as a playmaker who helped his teammates get good shots. Pete Maravich was also proud of his passing. However, most fans remember him for his amazing scoring records. Pistol Pete averaged more than 40 points a game as a college sophomore, junior, and senior during the 1960s.

No one has ever had a higher scoring average than Wilt Chamberlain. During the 1961–62 NBA season, he averaged 50.4 points per game for the Philadelphia Warriors. During that unforgettable season, Chamberlain also became the first (and only) player to score 100 points in an NBA game. The Warriors were playing the Knicks. The big center was unstoppable that night. After three quarters, Chamberlain had 69 points. The crowd started yelling, "Give it to Wilt! Give it to Wilt!" His teammates did just that.

Cheryl Miller drives to the hoop during her days as a college star for the University of Southern California.

With 46 seconds left in the fourth quarter, he scored his 100th point.

Two college players have scored 100 points in a game. The first was Bevo Francis, who played for Rio Grande Junior College in Texas. Francis was very tall and had a very good shot. In 1953 he scored 116 points against Ashland Junior College—including 55 points in the final ten minutes! In 1954 Francis scored 113 against Hillsdale College. Hillsdale used three players to guard Francis, but he was just too tall and too good.

The second college player to score 100 points was Frank Selvy of Furman University. During a game against Newberry College in 1954, Selvy's teammates kept passing him the ball. The game was on television in Selvy's hometown, and his coach wanted to give the young man a night to remember. Instead, Selvy gave the *fans* an unforgettable night. He made 41 of his 66 shots and 18 free throws to finish with 100 points. Selvy scored his last 2 points on a long shot just as the final buzzer went off.

Scoring 100 points is a remarkable feat at any level— not just in college and the pros. Lisa Leslie and Cheryl Miller did it while playing in high school. No one was surprised when they became two of the greatest players in the history of women's basketball. NBA stars Dajuan Wagner and Drazen Petrovic also scored 100 points. Wagner did it in high school. Petrovic did it while playing for a professional team in Zagreb, Yugoslavia.

Part of the fun of watching basketball is knowing that a player or team can set a scoring record at any time. During the 1983–84 season, fans in Denver watched their Nuggets wage an exciting duel with the Detroit Pistons. After 48 minutes, the score

Blaze-ing a Path

Few players did more for women's basketball than Carol Blazejowski (*right*). A star in the 1970s and 1980s, she often scored 40 points a game. Her thrilling drives to the basket made her the most exciting player in college basketball. In 1977 more than 12,000 fans bought tickets to watch her play in New York's Madison Square Garden. Blaze scored 52 points that night.

was tied 145–145. The teams played three overtime periods before the Pistons won 186–184. It was the highest-scoring game in NBA history. In 1992 no one could believe their eyes when they saw the score of the game between Troy University and DeVry Institute. Troy won the game 258–141.

The fans at that game probably would have fallen asleep during a 1950 contest between the Lakers and Pistons. This was in the days before the shot clock, and the Pistons thought the best "defense" against the Lakers was to keep the ball for themselves. The strategy worked. The Pistons held the ball for minutes at a time and won 19–18.

By 1973 the NBA had the 24-second clock. However, college games still had not adopted a shot clock. That year the University of Tennessee and Temple University played a game of "stall ball" that ended with a score of 11–6. Tennessee won on the strength of four free throws in the second half. Neither team scored a basket in the final 20 minutes. Tennessee's players had so much energy afterward that they decided to stay in the gym and play an intrasquad game!

6 *For the Record*

BASKETBALL'S GREATEST SCORING MARKS

You may have heard the old saying that records are "made to be broken." As of 2008, these are the records that the top men and women in the pros will be shooting for.

MEN'S PROFESSIONAL RECORDS

Most Points

IN A QUARTER	33	George Gervin (*left*)	1977–78
IN A HALF	59	Wilt Chamberlain	1961–62
IN A SEASON	4,029	Wilt Chamberlain	1961–62
IN A CAREER	30,387	Kareem Abdul-Jabbar	1969–70 to 1988–89

Most Points in a Game

BY A GUARD	81	Kobe Bryant	2005–06
BY A FORWARD	71	Elgin Baylor	1960–61
BY A CENTER	100	Wilt Chamberlain	1961–62

Most Points in a Playoff Game

BY A GUARD	63	Michael Jordan	1986
BY A FORWARD	61	Elgin Baylor (*top right*)	1962
BY A CENTER	56	Wilt Chamberlain	1962

Highest Season Scoring Average

BY A GUARD	37.1	Michael Jordan	1986–87
BY A FORWARD	35.6	Rick Barry	1966–67
BY A CENTER	50.4	Wilt Chamberlain	1961–62

Highest Career Scoring Average

BY A GUARD	30.1	Michael Jordan
BY A FORWARD	27.4	Elgin Baylor
BY A CENTER	30.1	Wilt Chamberlain

Best Season Shooting Percentage

BY A GUARD	57.4	John Stockton (*bottom right*)	1987–88
BY A FORWARD	60.1	Cedric Maxwell	1979–80
BY A CENTER	72.7	Wilt Chamberlain	1972–73

Best Career Shooting Percentage

BY A GUARD	52.3	Maurice Cheeks	1978–79 to 1992–93
BY A FORWARD	55.8	Bobby Jones	1974–75 to 1985–86
BY A CENTER	59.9	Artis Gilmore	1971–72 to 1987–88

Most Three-Pointers

IN A GAME	12	Kobe Bryant	2002–03
	12	Donyell Marshall	2004–05
IN A SEASON	269	Ray Allen	2005–06
IN A CAREER	2,560	Reggie Miller	1987–88 to 2004–05
IN A ROW	13	Brent Price	1995–96
	13	Terry Mills	1996–97

Most Free Throws

IN A QUARTER	16	Vince Carter	2005–06
IN A GAME	28	Wilt Chamberlain	1961–62
		Adrian Dantley	1983–84
IN A SEASON	840	Jerry West (*top left*)	1965–66
IN A CAREER	9,787	Karl Malone	1985–86 to 2003–04
IN A ROW	97	Micheal Williams	1992–93 to 1993–94

WOMEN'S PROFESSIONAL RECORDS

Most Points

IN A GAME	46	Katie Smith	2001
IN A SEASON	860	Diana Taurasi (*bottom left*)	2006
IN A CAREER	5,412	Lisa Leslie	1997 to 2006

Highest Scoring Average

IN A SEASON	25.3	Diana Taurasi	2006
IN A CAREER	22.3	Seimone Augustus	2006 to 2007

Highest Shooting Percentage

IN A SEASON	66.8	Tamika Raymond	2003
IN A CAREER	56.4	Alisa Burras	1999 to 2003

Best Free Throw Percentage

IN A SEASON	98.4	Eva Nemcova	1999
IN A CAREER	89.7	Eva Nemcova	1997 to 2001

Most Three-Pointers

IN A GAME	8	Diana Taurasi	2006
IN A SEASON	121	Diana Taurasi	2006
IN A CAREER	598	Katie Smith	1999 to 2007

7 *Crystal Ball*

THE FUTURE OF SHOOTING

When you see an NBA star shoot, you are watching a sort of "history lesson." Everything that player does is based on the successes and failures of one hundred years of experimenting. A player from the early days of basketball would be amazed by today's shooters. A century ago, the best shooters made only one of five shots they tried. In the first years of the NBA, the best shooters were lucky to make one out of three. Now the top shooters make more than half of their shots.

Like the best athletes in any sport, basketball players are always trying to improve. Every day in practice, they work on their dribbling, passing, and rebounding. Of course, they also work on their shooting. Usually, they experiment with tiny changes. When they find an adjustment that helps, they stick with it. If other players think the same change can help them, they try it too.

How well will players shoot in the future? The answer depends on another important part of basketball: defense. No matter how well players shoot, good defenders can usually stop them. A player who makes ten jump shots in a row during warm-ups might not make two in a row with a defender trying to bat the ball away.

For shooters to keep improving, they will have to learn new ways to find open shots. That means running faster and jumping higher. It also means learning new ways to break free from good defensive players. If shooters can stay a "step ahead" of the defense, they will continue to get better and better.

Will players ever make all (or almost all) of their shots? Probably not. To understand why, just look at the shot clock. With so little time to shoot, a team does not always get a wide-open look at the basket. Even the best shooters find themselves holding the basketball with time running out. They have no choice but to heave up a poor shot before the buzzer goes off. A good shooter will make some of these attempts, but never all of them.

Will there ever be a superscorer in basketball—someone so much better than everyone else that he or she smashes all the records? It has happened once, so it could happen again. In the 1960s, Wilt Chamberlain had the athletic skill of players six feet tall, but he stood 12 inches taller. He could outrun and outjump all the players big enough to guard him. He scored 40 or more points almost every game.

Picture a player Chamberlain's size with lightning-fast moves, great leaping ability, and an accurate shot from anywhere on the court. Who could stop him? Maybe no one—except someone else with similar size and skill. Basketball fans have not yet seen such a player. But that does not mean they never will.

LeBron James says he learned to shoot by watching videos of Michael Jordan. Are tomorrow's shooting stars learning from James today?

TV Time

What today's young basketball players see on television will play a big part in the future of shooting. How do we know this? Because that is how many current NBA stars learned the game. They grew up during the 1980s and 1990s watching highlights of dunks and three-point shots on TV. In turn, these were the shots that young players practiced as kids. The next generation of basketball players is now doing the same—only they are watching the game's greatest stars on high-definition widescreen TVs. Their crystal-clear view of the game will help them become even better shooters.

Resources

WEBSITES

Basketball Hall of Fame   www.hoophall.com
The official site of the Basketball Hall of Fame features information on the greatest players in basketball history, including their biographies and statistics.

JockBio   www.jockbio.com
The Web's most comprehensive biographical sports site features profiles of the top NBA and WNBA players, plus a daily list of their birthdays.

NBA   www.nba.com
The official site of the National Basketball Association features information on teams and players, plus statistics, NBA history, and the official NBA rules.

NCAA   www.ncaasports.com
The official site of the National Collegiate Athletics Association features information on both the men's game and women's game, including statistics and historical facts.

WNBA   www.wnba.com
The official site of the Women's National Basketball Association features information on teams and players, plus statistics, WNBA history, and the official WNBA rules.

BOOKS

- DK Publishing. *Basketball*. New York: DK Children, 2005.
- DK Publishing. *Basketball's Best Shots*. New York: DK Publishing, 2002.
- Dunning, Mark. *Basketball: Learn How to Put Speed in Your Step, Do the Drills, and Master All the Moves*. New York: Sterling Publishing, 2003.
- Editors of Sports Illustrated. *The Basketball Book*. New York: Sports Illustrated, 2007.
- Hubbard, Jan, and David J. Stern. *The Official NBA Encyclopedia*. New York: Doubleday, 2000.
- Kennedy, Mike. *Basketball*. Danbury, CT: Franklin Watts, 2003.
- Kramer, Sydelle. *Basketball's Greatest Players*. New York: Random House, 1997.
- Rutledge, Rachel. *Women of Sports: The Best of the Best in Basketball*. Minneapolis: Millbrook Press, 1998.
- Smith, Charles R. *Rim Shots*. New York: Puffin Books, 2000.
- Stewart, Mark. *Basketball: A History of Hoops*. Danbury, CT: Franklin Watts, 1999.
- Taragano, Martin. *Basketball Biographies*. Jefferson, NC: McFarland & Company, 1991.

Index

Page numbers in italics refer to illustrations.